5

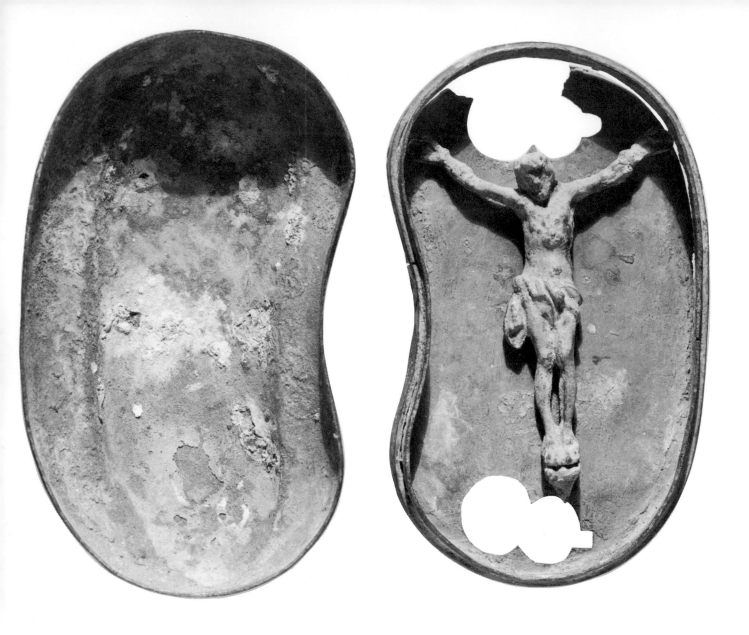

6

In the Beginning

I remember when I was born —
I do remember!
Through eternity I slept,
By its quiet waters swept,
In its silence safely kept.
All unknowing, night or day,
All unthinking, there I lay.
…Suddenly, by life compelled,
I was free, no longer held;
Free to hear and feel and cry;
Free to live — or free to die;
Free to be that which am I.
I remember when I was born —
I do remember!

The heart, it seems, can never know its age.
I would have said that at this stage,
I'd never love again.
 Yet here it is — the pain.
The ecstasy, the joy. . .
Against you I employ
My whole will to hide
Truth I have denied.

Words of Love
Pearl S. Buck

The John Day Company, New York

Book and jacket design by JEANYEE WONG

Copyright © 1974 by Creativity, Inc.

Library of Congress Cataloging in Publication Data

Buck, Pearl (Sydenstricker) 1892-1973.
    Words of love.

    Poems.
    I. Title.
PS3503.U198We   1974   811'.5'2   73-18535
ISBN 0-381-98263-7

The John Day Company, 257 Park Avenue South, New York, N.Y. 10010.

An Intext *Publisher*

Published on the same day in Canada by Longman Canada Limited.

Printed in the United States of America.

Dichotomy

Pilloried 'twixt heaven and hell,
my heart its secrets cannot tell.

Hung high upon a cross of praise,
my heart soul's saintliness betrays.

O Soul!

If rise you must, up from the dead,
leave heart behind in that cold bed.

You were a man,
I was a child,
You were a saint,
But I was wild.

Woman at last,
I saw too late
In your wise face,
The glimpse of fate.

How do I know?
Another face
Gazes at me
Across the space.

He sees me now
Too old — too old.
He is the child,
The young, the bold.

We travel on,
Alone and far,
Each in orbit,
Each a star.

Ask me no questions,
For I do not know
How into so many books
My lively dreams must grow.

Mine are dream-folk maybe —
Yet somehow they continue
In their own way, through me,
To wake and come alive.

Ask me no questions, pray!
There is no more to say.

You are me and I am you,
This I know is one thing true.

If you weep, then weep must I,
However otherwise I try.

If you laugh, then so must I,
However otherwise I try.

Laugh or weep, attuned to life
Let us put aside our strife.

11

Essence

I give you the books I've made,
Body and soul, bled and flayed.
Yet the essence they contain
In one poem is made plain;
In one poem is made clear:
On this earth, though far or near,
Without love there's only fear.

13

What are you to me?
You are my faith renewed
Lost through the years.
Yet now by faith imbued,
I cease my fears.

What are you to me?
A heart so quick and true
That my own heart,
Inured, is stirred anew
To do its part.

What are you to me?
A strong young source of power,
Who, with no strife,
But bringing seed to flower,
Infuses life.

The Quest

Love is a questing spirit,
Seeking where to find
A human frame to live in,
A human heart to bind.

A human heart to bind, dear love,
And so I offer mine.
Accept this heart and, if you will,
Use it as bread and wine.

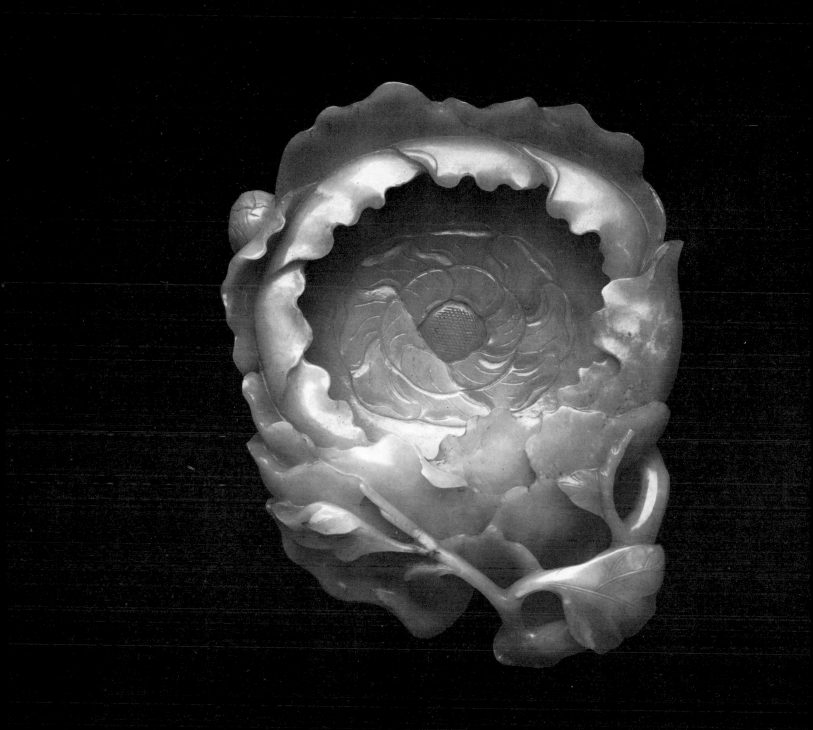

Item

Wonderful to love you
Wonderful to know
However far you wander,
There, too, my heart will go.

20

Conversation

"Return to me," I bade my Soul,
"Inhabit me again.
"Why wander on the wide round earth
"When heaven is your goal ?"

"Alas," my Soul to me replies.
"I am enslaved by Heart,
"Who follows that One whom it loves,
"And must, until it dies."

Question

You are not brave,
I am not brave,
Love's debt unpaid.
We are afraid
Lest we destroy
Our present joy.

I born too soon,
You born too late,
We two still wait.
Our times not matched,
Our hearts are latched.

Yet comes that day
I go, you stay.
I gone, you here —
What then, my dear?

Autumn

In autumn one must not allow
Heartbreak.
Sun sets behind the leaf-red bough.
The lake
Lies desolately bleak and chill.
I view
The empty land... O Heart, be still!
In lieu
Of love, accept the rule of will
And, cloaked in pride, go forth.
Now blows the wind forever from the north,
— Poor Heart! —

25

Fragment

Today my world is ended.
My heart no longer sings.
I fold my pride about me
As angels fold their wings.

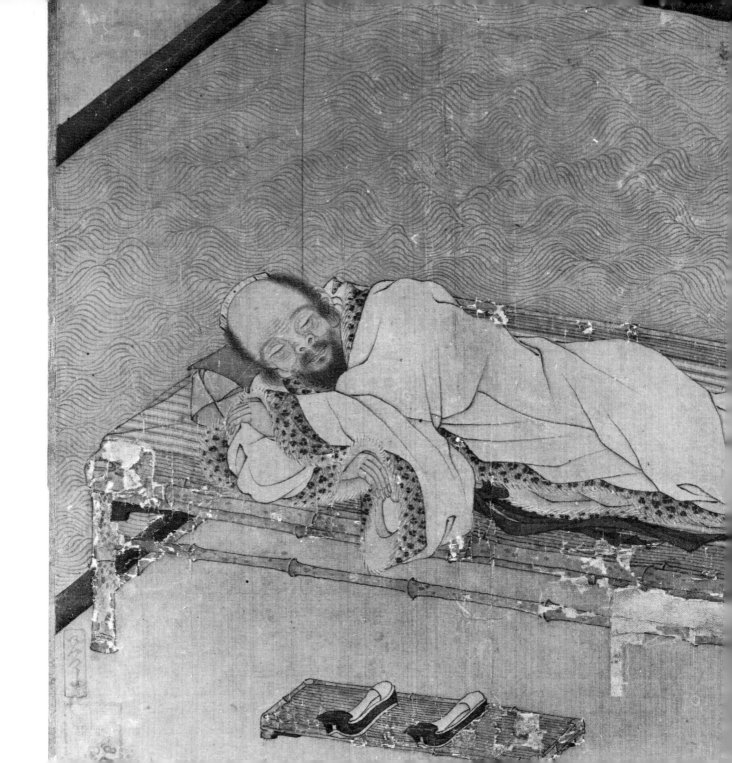

The Last Hour

Could you not watch with me
One last hour?
You with years in store, youth
Still in flower?
While here am I,
Doomed soon to die!

Not only His the loss,
Who, hung upon the cross,
Cried out against the cup,
Which now, alone, I sup!

30

Pretense

I put away the words of love.
You do not need them anymore.
And now I will pretend to be
Exactly as I was before.

Pretending, I will laugh and sing
Until night falls. Then to my shell
I'll creep and hide myself away,
Pretending heaven in my hell.

Desire

The slow rise, the swelling joy,
Filling vein and pulse until
Desire, flooding to its full height
Breaks — as breaks the wave upon
the sea.
Then am I you, love, and
You are me.

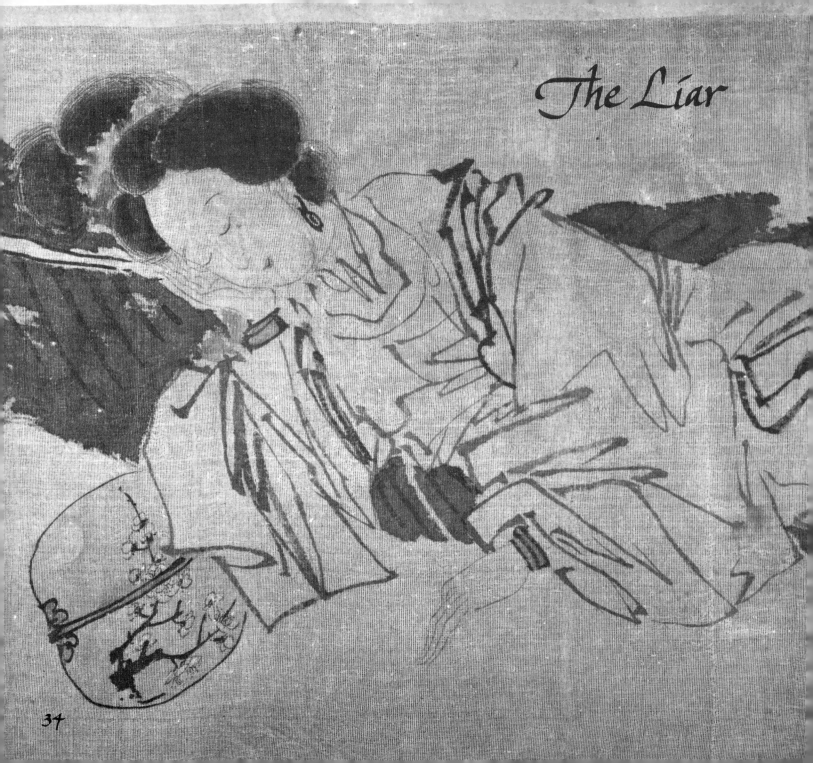

The Liar

34

In dreams I live,
In truth I die.
Therefore I dream,
Therefore I lie.

Myself alone
I do deceive.
That this is truth,
I will perceive.

I will perceive,
Yet dream the more,
For truth I hate,
And you adore.

Let Me Consider

Let me consider other joys,
I who have lived only for love.
Let me consider how the moon
Hangs high the mountaintop above,
And day by day, not late, not soon,
The bright sun swings across the sky.
Let me consider how birds fly
How goldfish dart across the pool —
Lest otherwise I play the fool!

To play the fool for love alone
Let heart instead be changed to stone.
And, cold of heart, but now at peace,
From love forever find release.

Freedom

At last we two are free,
I of you, you of me.
Love dying in its grave,
Silence is all I crave.

Alone

I am alone, myself in my own keeping,
Until the end. I, in my own grave sleeping,
Shall no longer hear your voice nor see your
face.
Yet shall I hear, yet see. In whatever
place
While my soul presses to new and lonely
birth,
You I shall hear, shall see, though you
Walk the earth.

41

Prayer

I pray you never know

How you have chosen ill

For good, small for great, low

For high. Therefore, I pray,

Sleep on until you wake

To find how lost your way!

Where is my home?
Where shall I find
True freedom for
The heart and mind?

What land contains
My people, who
Their dreams proclaim,
And make them true?

I live alone,
Through dreams I share.
The People? Ah,
They are not there!

45

Acknowledgments

Disk. Deeply carved with archaic dragons.
Ivory. *Ming Dynasty (1368–1644).*

3 THE METROPOLITAN MUSEUM OF ART, ROGERS FUND, 1919.

Wine Jar. (Hu). Bronze. *Han Dynasty (206 B.C.–A.D. 220).*

5 THE METROPOLITAN MUSEUM OF ART, BEQUEST OF WILLIAM MITCHELL, 1922.

Box with cover containing figure of Christ.
Bronze. *XV Century Ming Dynasty (1368–1644) (?).*

6 THE METROPOLITAN MUSEUM OF ART, GIFT OF MATHIAS KOMAR, 1951.

Pair of covered jars. White porcelain decorated
with underglaze blue. *K'ang-hsi Period (1662–1722).*
THE METROPOLITAN MUSEUM OF ART, BEQUEST OF MRS. H. O.

8 HAVEMEYER, 1929. THE H. O. HAVEMEYER COLLECTION.

Incense burner in shape of Mandarin ducks, symbol
of conjugal fidelity. Bronze. *Ming Dynasty (1368–1644) or earlier.*

11 THE METROPOLITAN MUSEUM OF ART, FLETCHER FUND, 1941.

Avalokitesvara (Kwannon) by an unknown Japanese
artist of the XV century or later. Colors on silk.
Copy of a painting by Yen Li-pen. *T'ang Dynasty (618–906).*

13 THE METROPOLITAN MUSEUM OF ART, GIFT IN MEMORY OF CHARLES STEWART SMITH, 1914.

Panel from border of twelve-panel screen by Fong Long,
Kon of Fatshan, 1690. Lacquer. *K'ang-hsi Period (1662–1722).*

14 THE METROPOLITAN MUSEUM OF ART, GIFT OF J. PIERPONT MORGAN, 1909.

Large dish: Nephrite. Jade. *Ming Dynasty (1368–1643).*

17 THE METROPOLITAN MUSEUM OF ART, GIFT OF HEBER R. BISHOP, 1902.

Head of a bodhisattva: Kuan Yin. Black marble. *Wei Dynasty (early VI century).*

19 THE METROPOLITAN MUSEUM OF ART, ROGERS FUND, 1917.

Double vase. Cloisonné enamel on copper.
K'ang-hsi Period (1662–1722).

20 THE METROPOLITAN MUSEUM OF ART, GIFT OF EDWARD KENNEDY, 1929.

"A Beauty" by unknown artist. *Sung Dynasty (960–1279).*
THE METROPOLITAN MUSEUM OF ART, BEQUEST OF MRS. H. O.

22 HAVEMEYER, 1929. THE H. O. HAVEMEYER COLLECTION.

25 Flowering hibiscus and white egret in autumn by Chao Tzu-ku (1199–1295). *Yuan Dynasty (1280–1368).*
THE METROPOLITAN MUSEUM OF ART, GIFT OF MRS. ANNA WOERISHOFFER, 1922.

26 Kuan Yin. Porcelain. *K'ang-hsi Period (1662–1722).*
THE METROPOLITAN MUSEUM OF ART, BEQUEST OF MARY STILLMAN HARKNESS, 1950.

28 Album leaf. "Sleeping Man" by unknown artist. Colors on silk. *Style of the Sung Dynasty (960–1279).*
THE METROPOLITAN MUSEUM OF ART, FLETCHER FUND, 1947. THE A. W. BAHR COLLECTION.

30 Group of figures with famille verte decoration. Porcelain. *K'ang-hsi Period (1622–1722).*
THE METROPOLITAN MUSEUM OF ART, GIFT OF EDWIN C. VOGEL, 1963.

32 Vase. Porcelain. *K'ang-hsi Period (1622–1722).*
THE METROPOLITAN MUSEUM OF ART, PURCHASE, 1879.

33 Hand scroll. Sleeping lady on a banana leaf. Attributed to T'ang Yin (1466–1524). Ink on silk. *Ming Dynasty (1368–1644).*
THE METROPOLITAN MUSEUM OF ART, FLETCHER FUND, 1947. THE A. W. BAHR COLLECTION.

36 Figure in landscape, artist unknown. Colors on silk. *Sung Dynasty (960–1279) or Ming Dynasty (960–1644).*
THE METROPOLITAN MUSEUM OF ART, GIFT OF MRS. MAURICE CASALIS, 1945.

38 Hand scroll attributed to Su Shih (1036–1101). Ink on paper. *Yuan Dynasty (1280–1368) or early Ming Dynasty (1368–1644).*
THE METROPOLITAN MUSEUM OF ART, FLETCHER FUND, 1947. THE A. W. BAHR COLLECTION.

41 Kuan Yin, seated. Painted wood. *Late Sung Dynasty (960–1279).*
THE METROPOLITAN MUSEUM OF ART, FLETCHER FUND, 1928.

42 Wine cup with swallow cover. Bronze. *Shang Dynasty (1766–1122 B.C.).*
THE METROPOLITAN MUSEUM OF ART, ROGERS FUND, 1943.

45 Classic gem attributed to Ch'iu Ying. *Ming Dynasty (1368–1644).*
THE METROPOLITAN MUSEUM OF ART, KENNEDY FUND, 1913.